W9-ALX-478

Finding Shapes

Triangles

Diyan Leake

Heinemann Library
Chicago, Illinois

© 2006 Heinemann Library
a division of Reed Elsevier, Inc.
Chicago, Illinois

Customer Service 888-454-2279
Visit our website at www.heinemannlibrary.com

Editorial: Diyan Leake
Design: Joanna Hinton-Malivoire
Photo research: Maria Joannou
Production: Chloe Bloom

Library of Congress Cataloging-in-Publication Data

Leake, Diyan.
    Triangles / Diyan Leake.
        p. cm. -- (Finding shapes)
    Includes index.
    ISBN 1-4034-7477-X (lib. bdg.) -- ISBN 1-4034-7482-6 (pbk.)
    1. Triangle--Juvenile literature. 2. Shapes--Juvenile literature. I.
Title. II. Series: Leake, Diyan. Finding shapes.
QA482.L437 2006
516'.154--dc22

                            2005013913

Printed and bound in China by South China Printing Co. Ltd

10 09 08 07 06
10 9 8 7 6 5 4 3 2 1

Acknowledgments
The author and publishers are grateful to the following for permission to reproduce copyright material: Aviation Images p. **16** (M. Wagner); Corbis pp. **6** (Sandro Vannini), **7**; Getty Images pp. **13** (Taxi/Eri Morita), **15** (Stone/Mitch Epstein), **18** (Botanica), **19** (Photodisc), back cover (boat, Botanica; slide, Taxi/Eri Morita); Harcourt Education Ltd pp. **5** (Malcolm Harris), **8** (Malcolm Harris), **9** (Tudor Photography), **10** (Malcolm Harris), **11** (Tudor Photography), **12** (Malcolm Harris), **17** (top & bottom, Tudor Photography), **20** (Tudor Photography), **21** (Tudor Photography), **22** (Tudor Photography), **23** (pyramid, Tudor Photography; straight, Malcolm Harris); Rex Features p. **14** (The Travel Library)

Cover photograph reproduced with the permission of Alamy

Every effort has been made to contact copyright holders of any material reproduced in this book. Any omissions will be rectified in subsequent printings if notice is given to the publishers.

The author and publisher would like to thank Patti Barber, specialist in Early Childhood Education, for her advice and assistance in the preparation of this book.

The paper used to print this book comes from sustainable resources.

Contents

What Is a Triangle?. 4

Where Can I See Triangles?. 6

Are There Triangles at Home?. 8

Can I See Triangles at School? 10

Are There Triangles Outside?. 14

Do Airplanes Have Triangles? 16

Do Boats and Ships Have Triangles? . . . 18

Can Triangles Be Part of

      Other Shapes? 20

Can I Go on a Triangle Walk?. 22

Picture Glossary 23

Index. 24

Some words are shown in bold, **like this**. They are explained in the glossary on page 23.

What Is a Triangle?

A triangle is a **flat** shape with three **corners**.

You can see flat shapes but you cannot pick them up.

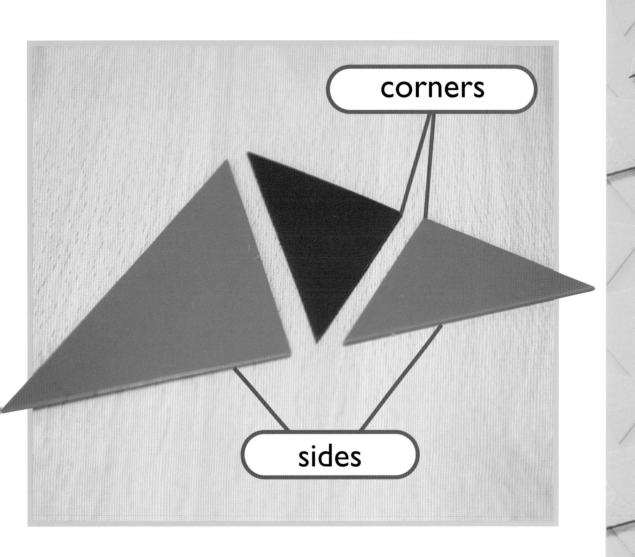

corners

sides

All triangles have three **sides**.

The sides are **straight**.

Where Can I See Triangles?

There are triangles all around us.

The top of a house may have a triangle shape.

The **sides** of a triangle are not always the same length.

Are There Triangles at Home?

We can cut some food into triangle shapes.

We can fold paper napkins into triangles.

These pieces of cheese are cut in a triangle shape.

Can I See Triangles at School?

There are small triangles and big triangles at school.

These triangles are small enough to hold.

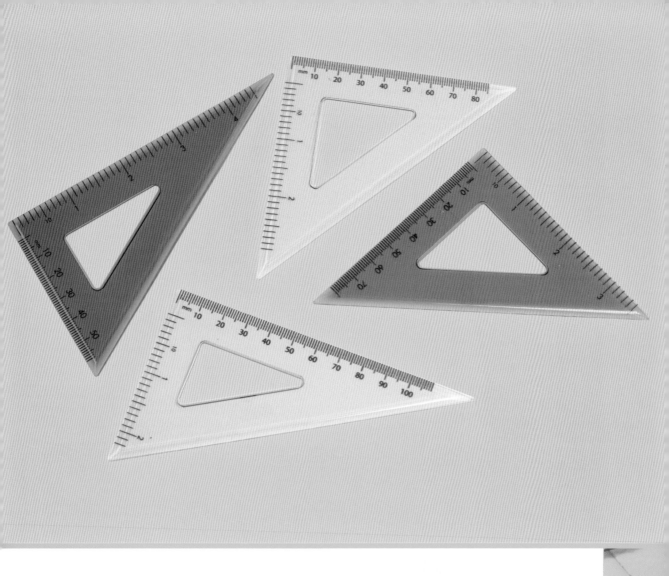

These triangles are good for drawing **straight** lines and **corners**.

What big triangles are there at school?

This climber has triangles on it.

The net inside the frame is made of red plastic rope.

The frame of a slide has a triangle.

You slide down one **side** of the triangle.

Are There Triangles Outside?

Parts of these tents are triangles.

People sleep in tents when they go camping.

These triangles are blowing in the wind.

They are red, white, and blue.

Do Airplanes Have Triangles?

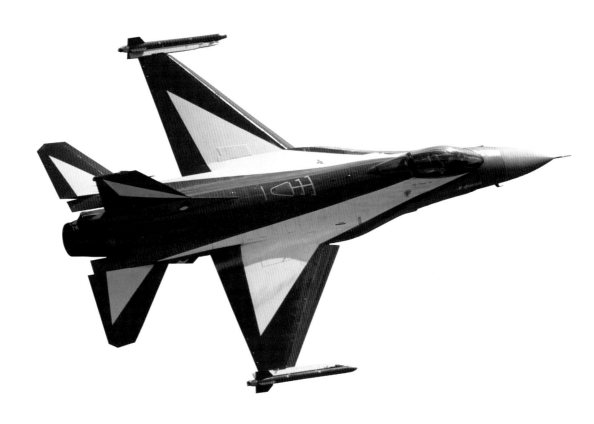

This airplane has triangles on its wings.

It is zooming across the sky.

You can fold paper into
an airplane.

The wings of a paper airplane
have a triangle shape.

Do Boats and Ships Have Triangles?

Some boats have sails in the shape of a triangle.

The wind fills the sails to move the boat along.

Ships may have flags of different colors on them.

Some of the flags are triangles.

Can Triangles Be Part of Other Shapes?

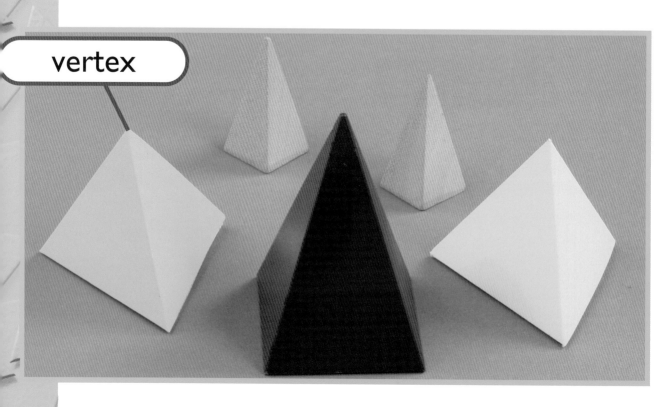

vertex

Triangles can be part of a shape called a **pyramid**.

All the triangles in a pyramid meet at one **vertex**.

20

The bottom of a pyramid can be a triangle.

It can sometimes be a **square**.

21

Can I Go on a Triangle Walk?

Walk around the playground and see how many triangles you can find!

Picture Glossary

corners
parts of a shape where two sides come together

flat
having no thickness

pyramid
shape that has triangles that all come together at one vertex

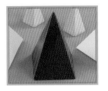
sides
outside lines of a flat shape

square
flat shape with four corners and four straight sides that are all the same size

straight
not bent or curved

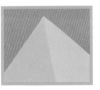
vertex
corner of a shape

Index

airplanes   16, 17

boats and ships   18, 19

cheese   9

climbers   12

corners   4, 11, 23

flags   19

food   8, 9

houses   6

paper napkins   8

pyramids   20, 21, 23

sails   18

sides   5, 7, 13, 23

slides   13

squares   21, 23

tents   14

vertex   20, 23

Note to Parents and Teachers

Reading nonfiction texts for information is an important part of a child's literacy development. Readers can be encouraged to ask simple questions and then use the text to find the answers. Each chapter in this book begins with a question. Read the questions together. Look at the pictures. Talk about what the answer might be. Then read the text to find out if your predictions were correct. To develop readers' inquiry skills, encourage them to think of other questions they might ask about the topic. Discuss where you could find the answers. Assist children in using the contents page, picture glossary, and index to practice research skills and new vocabulary.